EASY POP MELODIES
FOR OCARINA

ISBN 978-1-5400-2675-0

Visit Hal Leonard Online at
www.halleonard.com

Contact Us:
Hal Leonard
7777 West Bluemound Road
Milwaukee, WI 53213
Email: info@halleonard.com

In Europe contact:
Hal Leonard Europe Limited
Distribution Centre, Newmarket Road
Bury St Edmunds, Suffolk, IP33 3YB
Email: info@halleonardeurope.com

In Australia contact:
Hal Leonard Australia Pty. Ltd.
4 Lentara Court
Cheltenham, Victoria, 3192 Australia
Email: info@halleonard.com.au

BELIEVER

Words and Music by DANIEL REYNOLDS, WAYNE SERMON,
BEN McKEE, DANIEL PLATZMAN, JUSTIN TRANTOR,
MATTIAS LARSSON and ROBIN FREDRICKSSON

CANDLE IN THE WIND

Words and Music by ELTON JOHN
and BERNIE TAUPIN

CLOCKS

Words and Music by GUY BERRYMAN,
JON BUCKLAND, WILL CHAMPION
and CHRIS MARTIN

Moderately

The lights go out and I can't be saved. __ Tides that I tried to
Con - fu - sion nev - er stops, __ clos - ing walls and

swim a - gainst __ have brought me down up - on my knees. __
tick - ing clocks. __ Gonna come back and take you home. __ I

Oh, I beg, I beg and plead, __ sing - ing... Come out of
could not stop; that you know now, __ sing - ing... Come out up -

things un - said. __ Shoot an ap - ple off my head, __ and a,
on my seas. __ Curse missed op - por - tu - ni - ties. __ Am I

trou - ble that can't be named. __ A ti - ger's wait - ing
a part of the cure, __ or am I part of

to be tamed, __ sing - ing...} You _____ are. __
the dis - ease, __ sing - ing...}

_____ You _____ are. __

EDELWEISS
from THE SOUND OF MUSIC

Lyrics by OSCAR HAMMERSTEIN II
Music by RICHARD RODGERS

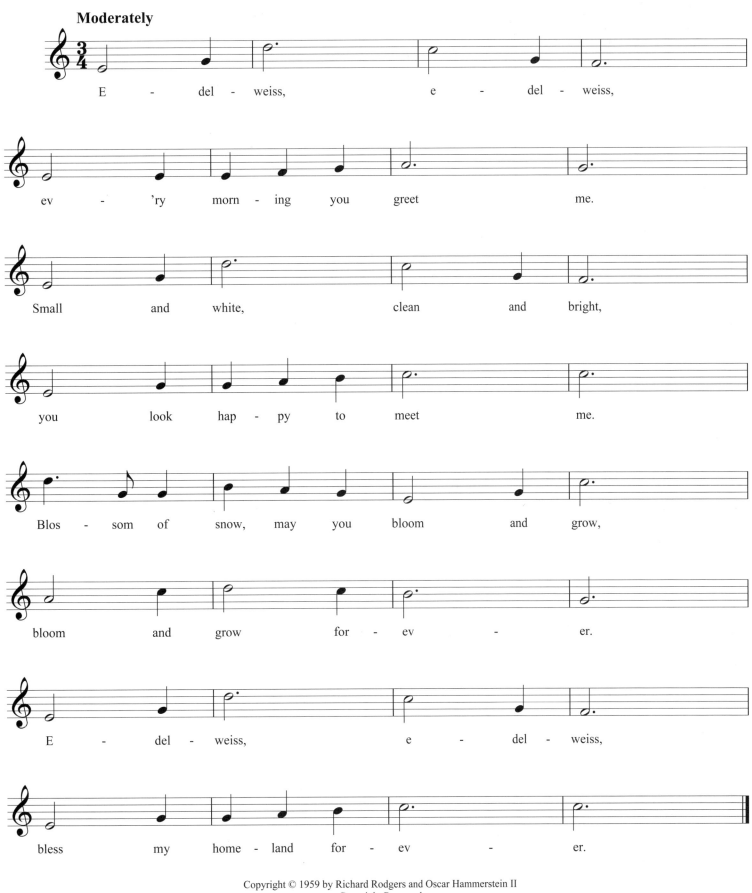

EVERY BREATH YOU TAKE

Music and Lyrics by
STING

(Everything I Do)
I DO IT FOR YOU

from the Motion Picture ROBIN HOOD: PRINCE OF THIEVES

Words and Music by BRYAN ADAMS,
R.J. LANGE and MICHAEL KAMEN

HALLELUJAH

Words and Music by
LEONARD COHEN

HAPPY
from DESPICABLE ME 2

Words and Music by
PHARRELL WILLIAMS

Moderately fast

(small note optional)

It might seem cra - zy what I'm 'bout to say:

Sun - shine _ she's here; _ you can take a break. I'm a

hot air bal - loon _____ that could go to space with the air _

_ like I don't care, _ ba - by by the way. _____ (Be - cause I'm

hap - py.) Clap a - long if _____ you feel _ like a room with - out a roof. _ (Be - cause I'm

hap - py.) Clap a - long if _____ you feel _ like hap - pi - ness is the truth. _ (Be - cause I'm

hap - py.) Clap a - long _____ if _____ you know _ what hap - pi - ness is to you. _ (Be - cause I'm

hap - py.) Clap a - long if _____ you feel _ like that's what you wan - na do. _____

HEY, SOUL SISTER

Words and Music by PAT MONAHAN,
ESPEN LIND and AMUND BJORKLAND

I'M YOURS

Words and Music by
JASON MRAZ

LET IT BE

Words and Music by JOHN LENNON
and PAUL McCARTNEY

LET IT GO

Words and Music by JAMES BAY
and PAUL BARRY

THE LION SLEEPS TONIGHT

New Lyrics and Revised Music by GEORGE DAVID WEISS,
HUGO PERETTI and LUIGI CREATORE

MORNING HAS BROKEN

Words by ELEANOR FARJEON
Music by CAT STEVENS

MY GIRL

Words and Music by SMOKEY ROBINSON
and RONALD WHITE

MY HEART WILL GO ON
(Love Theme from 'Titanic')

from the Paramount and Twentieth Century Fox Motion Picture TITANIC

Music by JAMES HORNER
Lyric by WILL JENNINGS

PERFECT

Words and Music by
ED SHEERAN

ROLLING IN THE DEEP

Words and Music by ADELE ADKINS
and PAUL EPWORTH

ROAR

Words and Music by KATY PERRY,
MAX MARTIN, DR. LUKE,
BONNIE McKEE and HENRY WALTER

SAY SOMETHING

Words and Music by IAN AXEL,
CHAD VACCARINO and MIKE CAMPBELL

Very slowly, in 4

SHAKE IT OFF

Words and Music by TAYLOR SWIFT,
MAX MARTIN and SHELLBACK

SOME NIGHTS

Words and Music by JEFF BHASKER,
ANDREW DOST, JACK ANTONOFF
and NATE RUESS

THE SOUND OF SILENCE

Words and Music by
PAUL SIMON

STAY WITH ME

Words and Music by SAM SMITH,
JAMES NAPIER, WILLIAM EDWARD PHILLIPS,
TOM PETTY and JEFF LYNNE

SWEET CAROLINE

Words and Music by
NEIL DIAMOND

UPTOWN GIRL

Words and Music by
BILLY JOEL

VIVA LA VIDA

Words and Music by GUY BERRYMAN,
JON BUCKLAND, WILL CHAMPION
and CHRIS MARTIN

WHAT A WONDERFUL WORLD

Words and Music by GEORGE DAVID WEISS
and BOB THIELE

YESTERDAY

Words and Music by JOHN LENNON
and PAUL McCARTNEY

YOU'VE GOT A FRIEND

Words and Music by
CAROLE KING

12-Hole Ocarina Fingering Chart

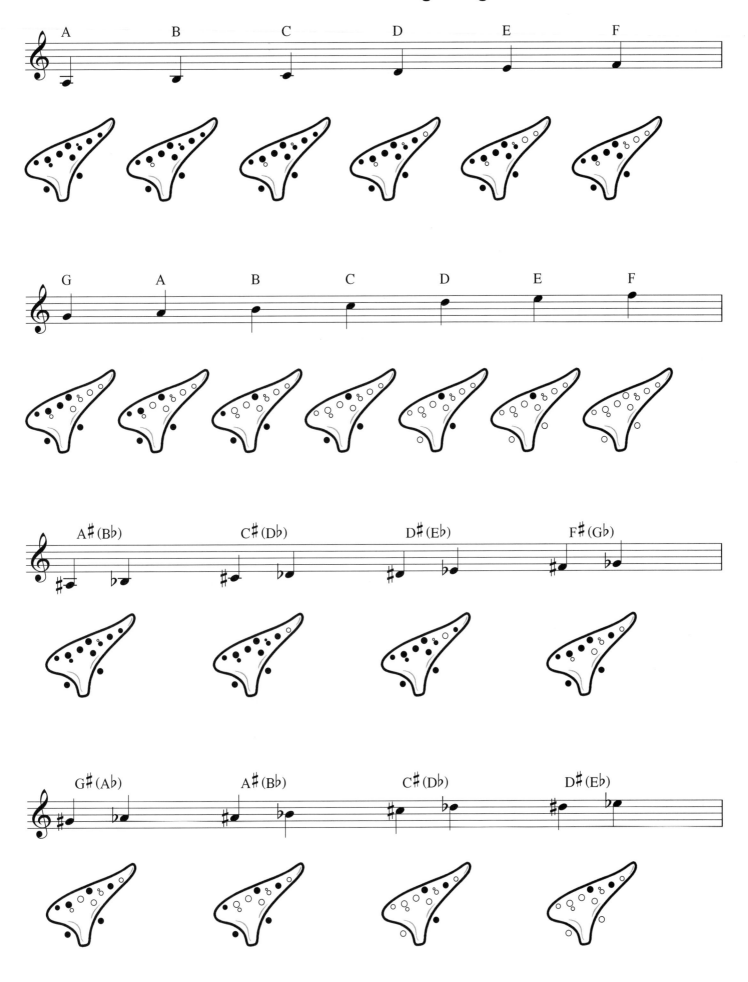

MORE GREAT OCARINA PUBLICATIONS

Christmas Carols for Ocarina

Arranged for 10, 11 & 12-Hole Ocarinas

30 favorite carols of the holiday season: Angels We Have Heard on High • Away in a Manger • Coventry Carol • Deck the Hall • God Rest Ye Merry, Gentlemen • It Came upon the Midnight Clear • Jingle Bells • Joy to the World • O Come, All Ye Faithful • O Holy Night • Silent Night • Up on the Housetop • We Wish You a Merry Christmas • and more.

00277990 ....$9.99

Christmas Favorites for Ocarina

Arranged for 10, 11 & 12-Hole Ocarinas

Play 23 holiday classics in arrangements tailored to this unique wind instrument: Blue Christmas • Christmas Time Is Here • Do You Hear What I Hear • Frosty the Snow Man • Have Yourself a Merry Little Christmas • The Little Drummer Boy • The Most Wonderful Time of the Year • Rockin' Around the Christmas Tree • Silver Bells • White Christmas • Winter Wonderland • and more.

00277989 ....$9.99

Disney Songs for Ocarina

Arranged for 10, 11 & 12-Hole Ocarinas

30 Disney favorites, including: Be Our Guest • Can You Feel the Love Tonight • Colors of the Wind • Do You Want to Build a Snowman? • Evermore • He's a Pirate • How Far I'll Go • Kiss the Girl • Lava • Mickey Mouse March • Seize the Day • That's How You Know • When You Wish Upon a Star • A Whole New World • You've Got a Friend in Me • Zip-A-Dee-Doo-Dah • and more..

00275998 .... $10.99

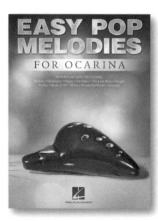

Easy Pop Melodies for Ocarina

Arranged for 10, 11 & 12-Hole Ocarinas

30 popular hits: Believer • City of Stars • Every Breath You Take • Hallelujah • Happy • I'm Yours • The Lion Sleeps Tonight • My Heart Will Go on (Love Theme from *Titanic*) • Perfect • Rolling in the Deep • Shake It Off • Some Nights • The Sound of Silence • Stay with Me • Sweet Caroline • Uptown Girl • What a Wonderful World • Yesterday • You've Got a Friend • and more.

00275999 .... $9.99

Folk Songs for Ocarina

Arranged for 10, 11 & 12-Hole Ocarinass

41 well-known songs: Alouette • Aura Lee • The Banana Boat Song • Follow the Drinkin' Gourd • Frere Jacques (Are You Sleeping?) • Hava Nagila (Let's Be Happy) • Home on the Range • Hush, Little Baby • Joshua (Fit the Battle of Jericho) • Kumbaya • La Cucaracha • Loch Lomond • My Bonnie Lies over the Ocean • My Old Kentucky Home • My Wild Irish Rose • Oh! Susanna • Scarborough Fair • Shenandoah • Swing Low, Sweet Chariot • This Little Light of Mine • Twinkle, Twinkle Little Star • Volga Boatman Song • When Johnny Comes Marching Home • The Yellow Rose of Texas • and more.

00276000 ....$9.99

Hal Leonard Ocarina Method
by Cris Gale

The Hal Leonard Ocarina Method is a comprehensive, easy-to-use beginner's guide, designed for anyone just learning to play the ocarina. Inside you'll find loads of techniques, tips and fun songs to learn and play. The accompanying online video, featuring author Cris Gale, provides further instruction as well as demonstrations of the music in the book. Topics covered include: a history of the ocarina • types of ocarinas • breathing and articulation • note names and key signatures • meter signatures and rhythmic notation • fingering charts • many classic folksongs • and more.

00146676 Book/Online Video $14.99

Ocarina Songs for All Occasions

Arranged for 10, 11 & 12-Hole Ocarinas
arr. Cris Gale

30 songs for every season: America, the Beautiful • Auld Lang Syne • Danny Boy • Hail to the Chief • Happy Birthday to You • Joy to the World • The Old Rugged Cross • Pomp and Circumstance • Sevivon • The Star-Spangled Banner • Wedding March (Bridal Chorus) • When the Saints Go Marching In • and more.

00323196 ....$9.99

WWW.HALLEONARD.COM

Prices, contents, and availability subject to change without notice.
Disney characters and artwork TM & © 2021 Disney